I SPY
with my little eye...

OCEAN ANIMALS

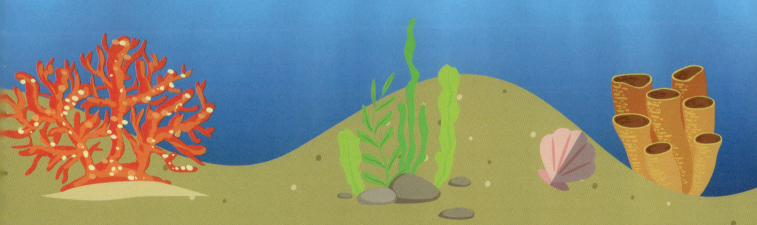

I spy with my little eye something beginning with...

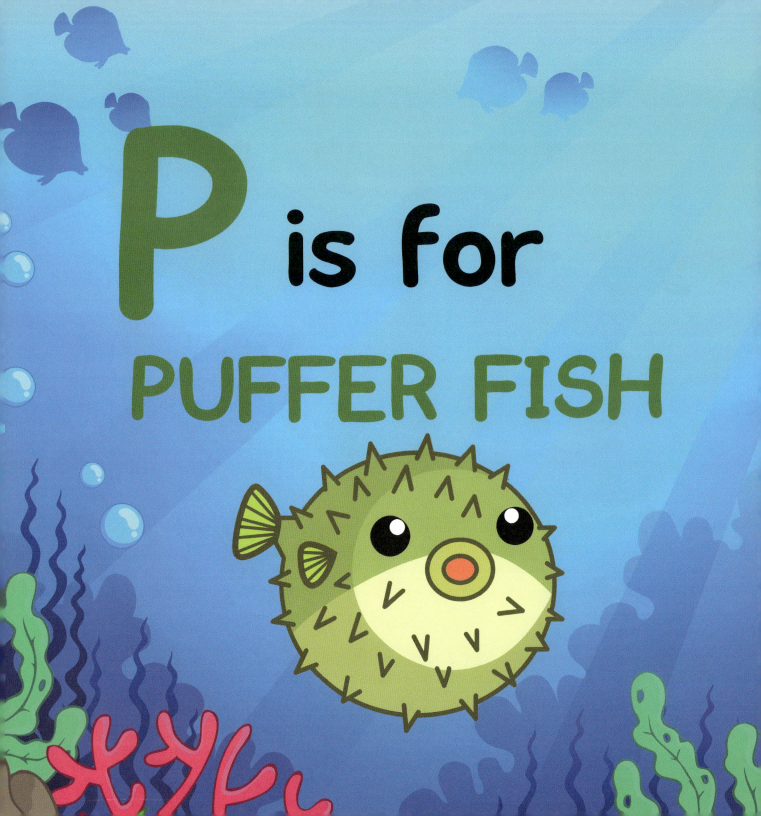

I spy with my little eye something beginning with...

T is for TURTLE

I spy with my little eye something beginning with...

D is for DOLPHIN

I spy with my little eye something beginning with...

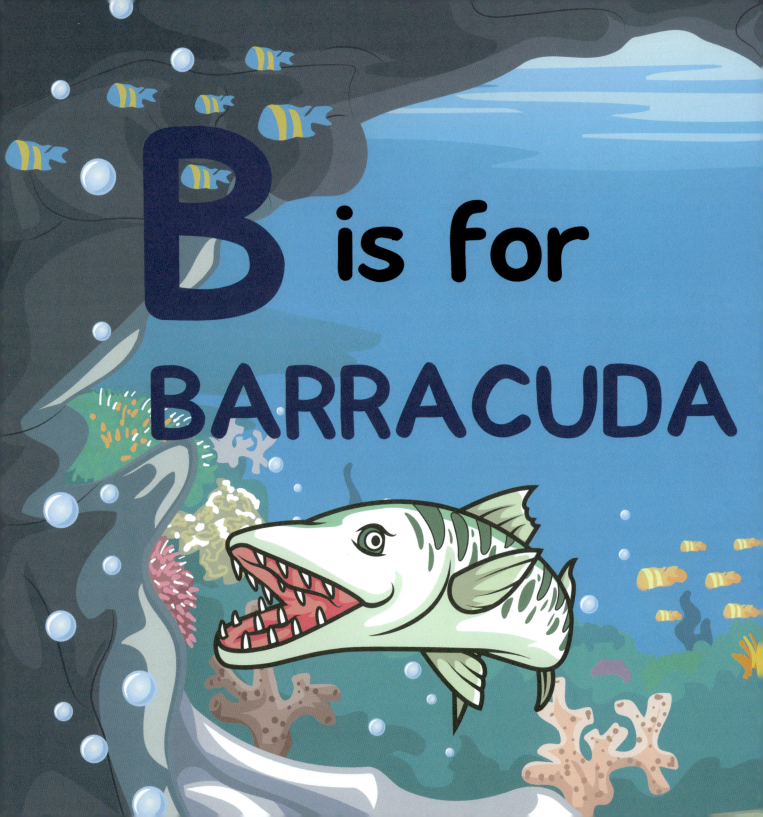

I spy with my little eye something beginning with...

I spy with my little eye something beginning with...

I spy with my little eye something beginning with...

I spy with my little eye something beginning with...

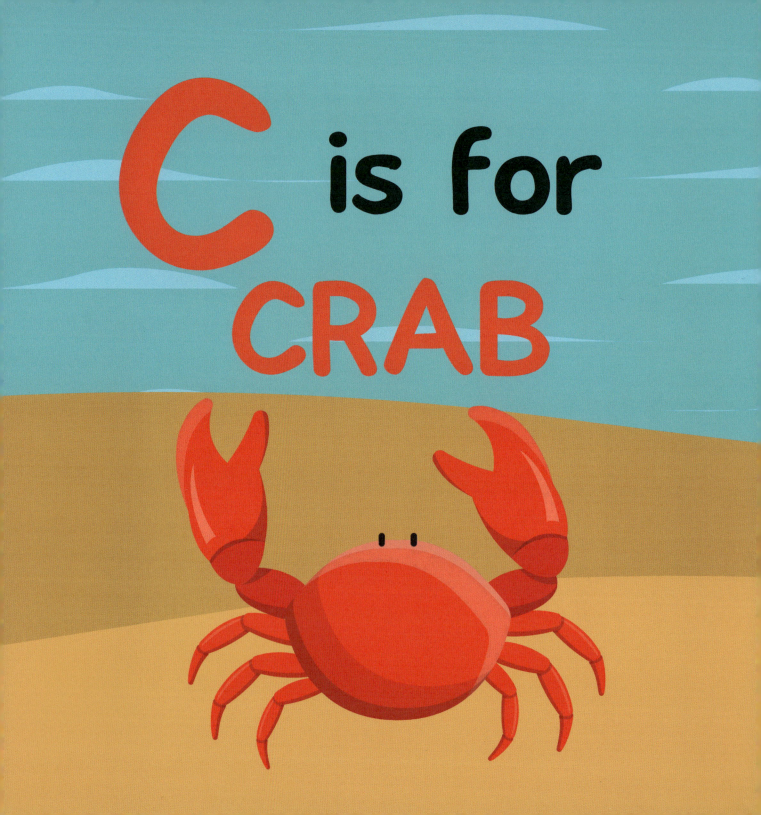

I spy with my little eye something beginning with...

I spy with my little eye something beginning with...

I spy with my little eye something beginning with...

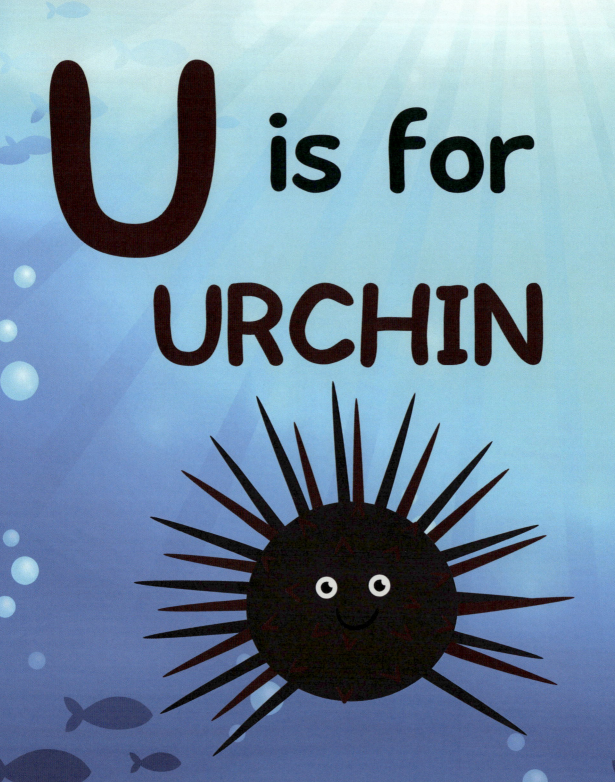

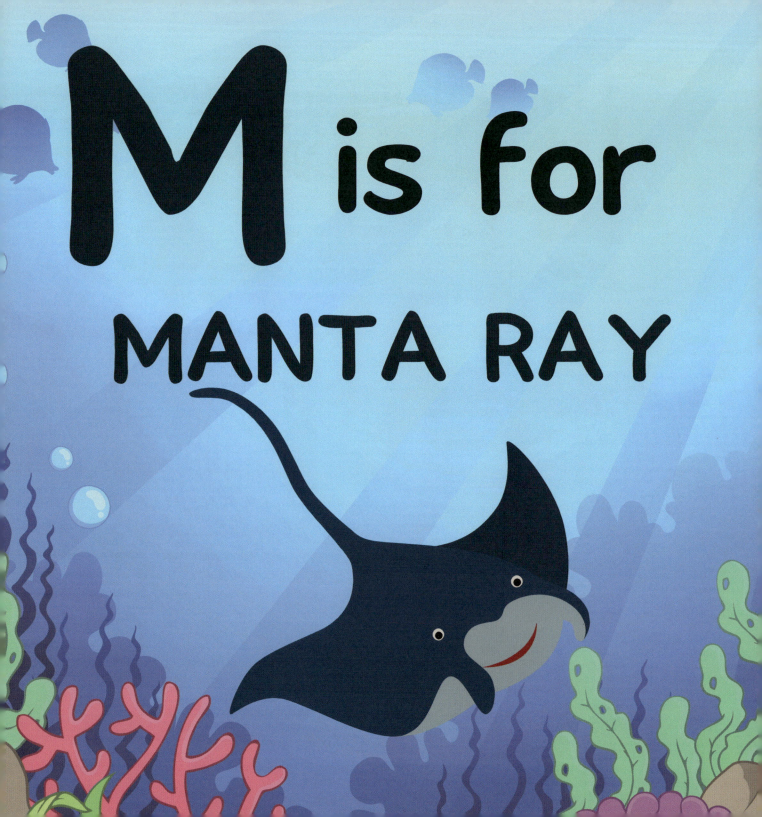

I spy with my little eye something beginning with...

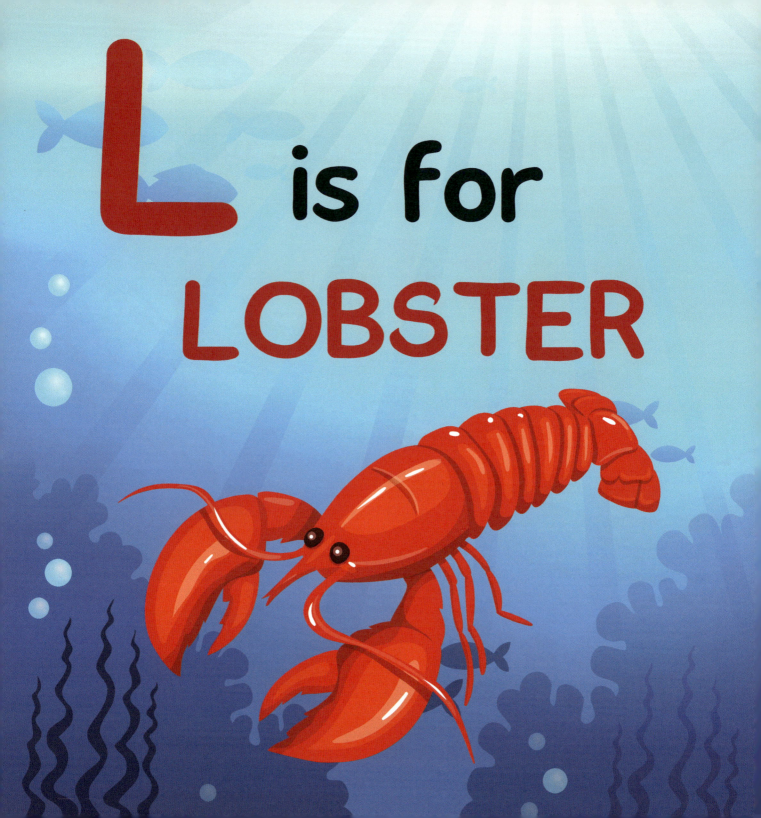

I spy with my little eye something beginning with...

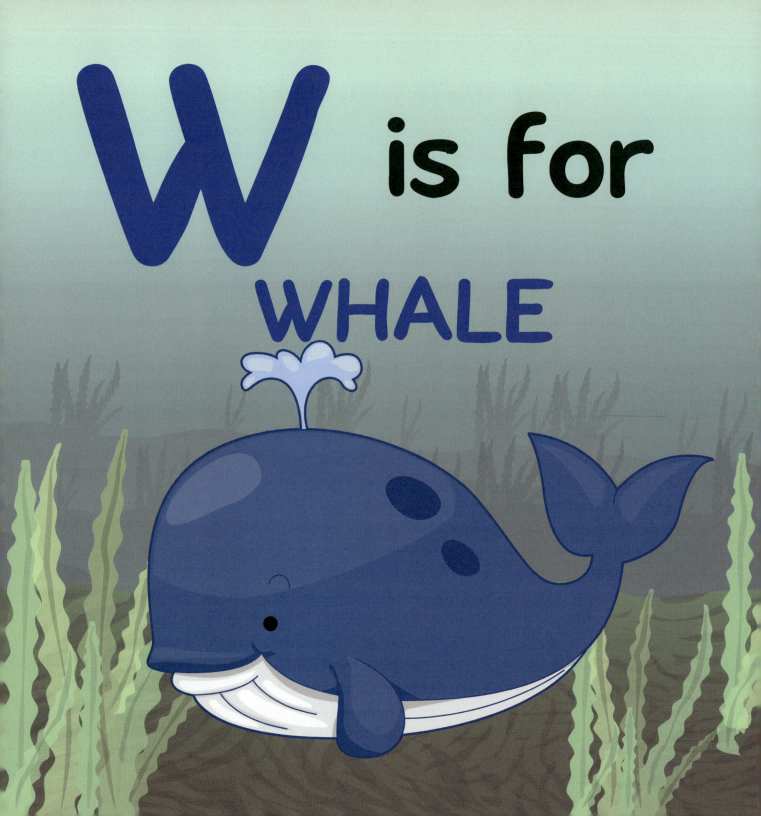

See our other products

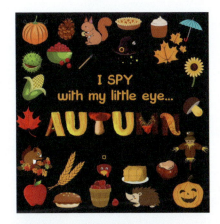
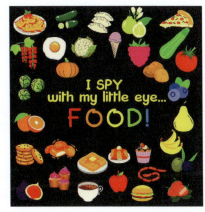
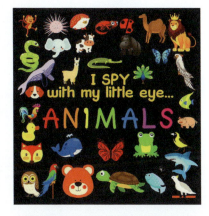

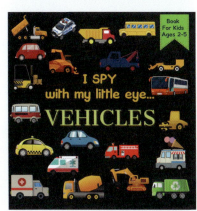

https://amzn.to/3jmbs9t

Printed in Great Britain
by Amazon